Rob

by Cynthia Swain • illustrated by Anita DuFalla

Pam and Tam are at the mat.
Pam and Tam have Rob.
Rob is on the mat.

Rub Rob, Pam.
Rub Rob, Tam.

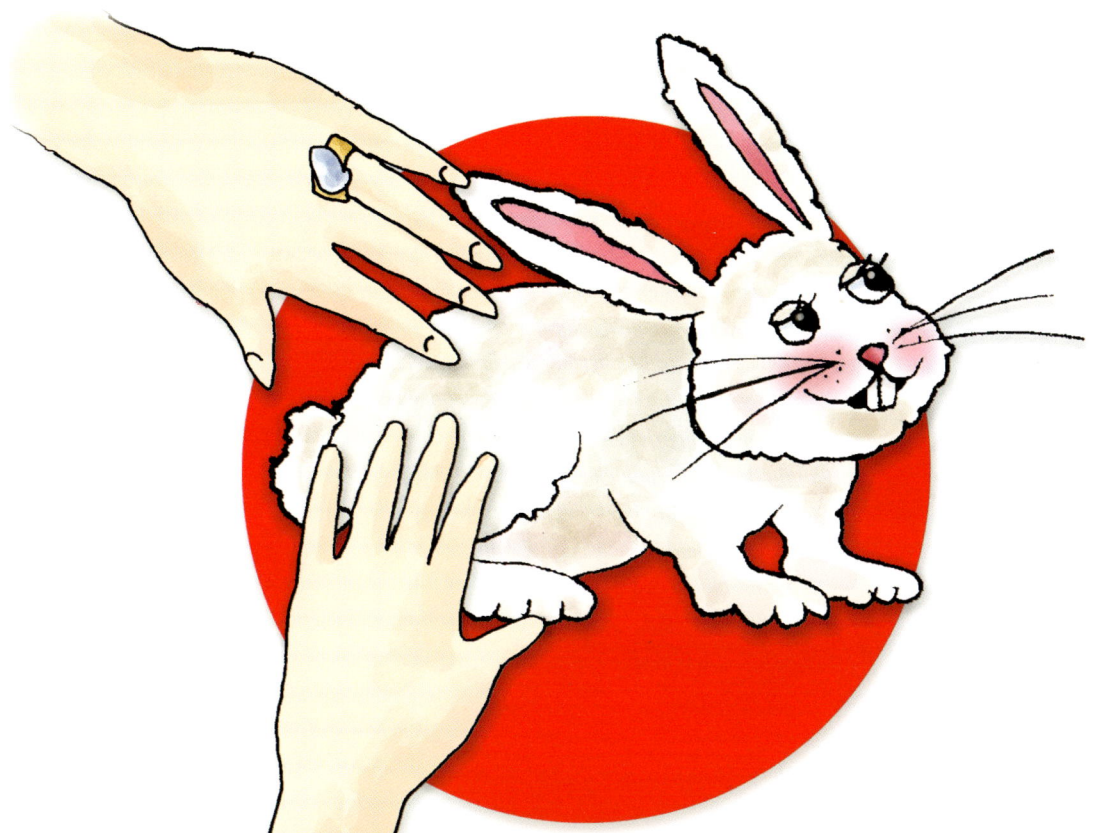

Rob can see the cat.
The cat is at the mat.

Rob ran. The cat ran.
Run, Pam and Tam!

Rob can see the pup.
The cat can see the pup.

The cat ran. The pup ran.
The cat and pup ran and ran.

Pam and Tam have Rob.
Rob is at the mat.